Oasis

Editor: **Mike Evans**
Assistant Editor: **Michelle Pickering**
Production Controller: **Michelle Thomas**
Picture Research: **Maria Gibbs**
Art Editor: **Penny Stock**
Design: **Design Revolution, Brighton**

Special thanks to:
Johnny, Christine and Karen at Creation Records

Record sleeve design & art direction by Brian Cannon for Microdot,
photography by Michael Spencer Jones

First published in 1995 by
Hamlyn, an imprint of
Reed Consumer Books Limited,
Michelin House, 81 Fulham Road,
London SW3 6RB
and Auckland, Melbourne, Singapore and Toronto

Copyright © 1995 Reed International Books Limited
and IPC Magazines Limited.

A Catalogue record for this book is available from the British Library
ISBN 0 600 58761 4

Printed in Hong Kong

Picture Acknowledgements

All Action/Gareth Davies 68 top

Apple Corps Ltd. 56

George Bowstead 21

Brian Cannon/Microdot 15, 23, 31, 41, 50, 51, 61, 75 below

Creation Records/Andy Wilsher 16 bottom

Steve Double 6-7,10

Fiona Hanson/PA News 68 bottom

Melody Maker 9 bottom, 12 bottom, 14,/**Piers Allardyce** 12 top,
/**George Bowstead** 70,/**Matt Bright** 80, **Joe Dilworth** 11 right,/**Grant
Peden** 13,/**Pat Pope** 5, 8, 44 top, 44 bottom, 48,/**Tom Sheehan** 17,
35, 36-37, 37 bottom, 38 left, 39, 40, 76 left/**Stephen Sweet** 9
top,/**Ian Tilton** 19 top,

Redferns/Mick Hutson 45, 46, 72 left, 74-75 top, 79, / **Steinwehe** 32

Retna/Steve Double 26, 28 top left, 28 top right,/**Tony Mottram** 22

Rex Features/Ph. J. Sutton - Hibbert 65 top right

S.I.N./Piers Allardyce 27 top,/**Martin Goodacre** 27 bottom,/
Hayley Madden 62,/**Tony Medley** 4, 53, 76 right, 77 bottom,/**Roy Tee**
55 bottom

Paul Slattery 3,16 top, 18 top centre, 18 top left, 18 top right, 19
centre, 19 bottom, 20, 24, 25 right, 25 left, 28 bottom, 29 bottom, 29
top right, 29 top left, 30, 33 bottom, 33 top, 34 bottom, 34 top, 36
left, 42-43, 47, 49, 52 bottom, 52 top, 54, 55 top, 57, 58, 59 bottom,
59 top, 60, 63 top, 63 bottom, 64, 65 bottom, 65 top left, 66 bottom,
66 top, 67, 69, 71, 73, 74 below, 77 top, 78

Oasis

PAUL LESTER

HAMLYN

CONTENTS

The Rain 5

'Supersonic' 15

'Shakermaker' 23

'Live Forever' 31

'Definitely Maybe' 41

'Cigarettes & Alcohol' 51

'Whatever' 61

Diary Of A Mad Rock Band 69

The Rain

'Your music's shite'

SIX

Manchester: so much to thank it for . . . the Gallagher brothers' delinquent teenage years . . . the baggy scene takes over in the city . . . Noel and Liam see The Stone Roses for the first time and find God . . . Noel roadies for Madchester's third band, The Inspiral Carpets . . .

Liam Gallagher: the most charismatic frontman since Ian Brown

MAN-CHEST-ER, LA LA LA

MANCHESTER, as Morrissey once pointed out, has a lot to answer for. Probably. Yet, crap weather and the odd bit of ugly architecture notwithstanding, it also has plenty to be grateful for, especially when it comes to music. For three decades, it has delivered the goods, bands-wise. From The Hollies and The Mindbenders to the vastly underrated 10cc to Simply Red to Take That to the stars of this book, the city has thrown up an extraordinary amount of talent.

In fact, with the obvious notable exceptions – The Sex Pistols, The Clash, The Jam and The Damned (London), ABC, Heaven 17, The Human League and Cabaret Voltaire (Sheffield), Orange Juice, Altered Images, The Fire Engines and Josef K (Glasgow), Frankie Goes To Hollywood, Teardrop Explodes, Echo And The Bunnymen and Wah! Heat (Liverpool) – it could easily be argued that the best, indeed the most important British groups of the last 20 years have come from this one Northern town.

The city's vibrant music scene really exploded into action in the wake of punk. Indeed, all subsequent generations of Manchester bands seem to have been the progeny of punk, in one way or another.

The seminal moment has to be the epochal occasion The Sex Pistols played the Manchester Free Trade Hall in autumn 1976. Everyone seemed to be in the audience on that fateful night – Pete Shelley and Howard Devoto, Paul Morley, Tony Wilson, Mark E Smith, Bernard Sumner and Peter Hook, and many more.

It wasn't long before said movers and shakers were making their own impression on the (music) world. Shelley and Devoto formed noise-pop romantics The Buzzcocks (Devoto later broke away to begin a rather more experimental adventure with Magazine), Morley became an influential *NME* writer and consistently championed local acts, Tony Wilson started Factory Records, Smith formed The Fall and the Sumner/Hook axis began the seminal Joy Division, who, after the suicide of singer Ian Curtis, metamorphosed into possibly the greatest (white dance) band on the entire planet, New Order.

After providing the mainstays of 'alternative' British rock for five or so years with the above groups as well as with A Certain Ratio, The Distractions and 52nd Street, Manchester entered a whole new creative period with the formation of The Smiths and James in 1982. Between 1983 and 1987, The Smiths and New Order (and, to a lesser extent, Cocteau Twins and The Jesus And Mary Chain) dominated the alternative pop world of the weekly music press and the indie charts.

But it was the arrival of two other bands in the late Eighties, and the scene that sprang up around them, which really provides the start of the Oasis story.

Now, Happy Mondays and The Stone Roses had actually been playing together

NINE

The Stone Roses at their peak, Alexandra Palace, November '89

and doing the odd, small local gig since the early-to-mid-Eighties (in fact, key player in the Oasis saga, *Melody Maker*'s Paul Mathur, wrote about Happy Mondays in the much-missed *Blitz* magazine as early as 1986 and the '*Maker* ran a cover story on them in March 1987), but it wasn't until 1988 that these two influential groups began to make a sizeable impression on 'the real world'.

By 1989, after the Roses and the Mondays had made a huge impact in Manchester, shockwaves were sent around the rest of the country where look-and-soundalike bands started coming out the woodwork of every conceivable provincial hellhole – The Charlatans, The High, Inspiral Carpets, The Mock Turtles (from Manchester and environs), and Blur (from Colchester), to name but five.

These bands were usually fronted by an Ian Brown (Stone Roses) or Shaun Ryder (Mondays) facsimile, all stoned nonchalance, indifferent, slurred vocals and sloppy, outsized gear. Their music also adopted the shuffling, loping beat of their mentors. Pretty soon, a word was coined to describe the music of these groups – baggy! – and another was invented to sum up the neo-psychedelic delirium of the period – Madchester.

Before long, thousands of Northern teenagers had seized upon this opportunity to discover clubs (notably, Manchester's legendary Hacienda), clothes (usually mega-baggy 'Joe Bloggs' tops and jeans), drugs (principally, Ecstasy) and music (primarily acid house – not for nothing have Oasis been described as 'the first band to speak for the post-rave generation').

For these bedazzled adolescents, Madchester was their Woodstock, their Sixties love'n'peace movement, their excuse

Sonic rebels The Jesus And Mary Chain

Oasis in classic Best Band In Britain mode (l-r): Paul 'Guigs' McGuigan, Tony McCarroll, Liam, Paul 'Bonehead' Arthurs and Noel

to go out and get drunk/high/laid. Affleck's Palace was their Biba, the Arndale Centre was their Carnaby Street and the Hacienda was their Roundhouse.

And, of course, The Stone Roses and Happy Mondays were, respectively, their Beatles and Rolling Stones: the Roses' mellifluous janglepop echoed that of their Sixties Liverpudlian antecedents, while the Mondays opted for the harsher sound, as well as the Last Gang In Town stance, of their southern forebears.

ROSES GROW ON YOU
IT was at one particularly memorable hometown Stone Roses show in early 1990 that the germ of the idea of forming a band probably first crossed the minds of the hugely impressed Liam and Noel Gallagher, the ('extremely lapsed Catholic') sons of Irish parents who were brought up in Burnage, a pleasant enough but dull suburb of South Manchester.

Not that Liam Gallagher, now 22 (he was born on September 22nd, 1972), had ever

King Baggy, the Roses' Ian Brown

Noel's first bosses in the music biz, Inspiral Carpets

The Smiths featuring Johnny Marr (far left), Noel's all-time guitar hero

been a big fan of music. No, the pubescent lothario was more into getting off with girls, as well as playing football and scoring draw, which he did for the first time when he was 14.

'I didn't give a fuck about music,' Liam says of his formative years. 'Anyone that walked past me with a guitar would get loads off me: "You fuckin' freak. You weirdo, playing music." I just thought it was all weird.'

On the other hand, Noel Gallagher, now 27, (born on May 29th, 1967), was into music. In the early Eighties, while his kid brother was still in short trousers, Noel discovered punk and its attendant don't-give-a-fuck attitude. Like many 14-year-olds in his area, he bunked off lessons, burgled a bit, snaffled various adhesives, drank copious quantities of cider and listened to The Sex Pistols.

'I was a bit of a rogue when I was young,' remembers Noel. 'I used to wag school and be into fuckin' glue-sniffing and stuff like that – no one was into smoking pot those days, and there was no Ecstasy or hard drugs like there are now. I was just completely out of fuckin' control – I didn't give a shit. Then,

Lad demi-gods, Happy Mondays

when I was 13, me and this lad robbed our corner shop, which is a very stupid thing to do cos everyone knows exactly who you are and where you live.'

As a result, Noel was put on probation and his parents grounded him for six months, a not entirely unfortunate punishment since it gave the elder Gallagher brother plenty of opportunity to practise on the acoustic guitar that his father, a Country & Western DJ (Noel: 'I used to help him set his gear up. I was like his roadie at the age of 10. All I remember is being given a Coke and a packet of crisps and being as bored as fuck'), had given him when he was 13 years old.

'I just sat there for six months playing one string on this acoustic guitar,' says Noel today. 'I thought I was really good for about a year until someone tuned it up. Then I thought, I can't play the fuckin' thing at all now. I'm gonna have to start all over again.'

Noel did start again, and pretty soon he had taught himself to play Beatles songs before the shocking realisation that, like his hero John Lennon, he was dyslexic.

'Somebody was playing a joke when they made me,' he looks back and laughs with a healthy self-derision. 'You know: "Let's make this guy a writer and a guitar player, but let's make him write with his left hand but play with his right."'

While still in his teens, Noel went to see The Smiths and was totally blown away by Johnny Marr's guitar-playing. Just as Marr's formative musical obsessions were George Harrison and the chiming 12-string Rickenbacker jangle of The Byrds' Roger McGuinn, Noel Gallagher now had his very own role model.

Yet, even after the impact of seeing The Stone Roses and being equally bowled over by guitarist John Squire's virtuoso fretboard runs, Noel Gallagher didn't really seriously entertain the notion of forming a band with 'such a moaning dick' as his own kid brother, the latter experiencing his personal Road To Damascus-type conversion to the whole rock'n'roll ethos the very second he clapped awestruck eyes on the lad demigod, Ian Brown.

CARPET BAGGER

BUT what did happen was that, at that very same Stone Roses concert, Noel approached someone who he had spotted taping the gig.

It turned out to be Clint Boon of the Inspiral Carpets, who, after the Roses and the Mondays, were the leading new band in the city. Discovering they had similar musical tastes, Noel and Clint soon became friends. Eventually, Gallagher was asked to be the Inspirals' guitar technician and roadie. Over the next two years, after quitting his job at British Gas, he got to travel the globe with the Carpets, visiting such far-flung places as Russia, Argentina, Japan and America.

It was while he was in America, in summer 1991, that Noel phoned home, only to be told by his mum (the brothers haven't seen their father in 10 years, although they remain close to their mother, the latter regularly 'clipping her sons around the ear' whenever they get too big for their boots) that Liam had joined a band, albeit mostly as a way of killing time in between trips to see his beloved Manchester City play.

Madchester's third band, the Inspirals

The band consisted of guitarist Paul 'Bonehead' Arthurs (the lunatic member of the group who was nicknamed thus after a particularly disastrous teenage haircut), bassist Paul 'Guigs' McGuigan (the increasingly lunatic member of the group) and drummer Tony McCarroll (the Quiet One). The three of them had been playing in a local band called The Rain (not to be confused with the Liverpudlian baggy bandwagon-jumpers of the same name) that had been going nowhere very slowly for quite a while.

But as soon as Liam (the Not Quiet At All One) joined The Rain as singer and frontman, the band at last snapped into action: they decided to change their name.

MIRAGE, MIRAGE ON THE WALL . . .

AFTER much brow-furrowing, the four lads came to a decision about their brand new monicker, one which, depending on which apocryphal story you believe, was taken from the name of a Manchester watering hole, from a local clothing emporium or from a poster on a street wall. The name was Oasis.

Noel may have been convinced that he never wanted to be in a band with his younger brother, but, back off tour with the Inspirals in January 1992, he did decide to check out Oasis' debut performance at Manchester's Boardwalk. He wasn't particularly impressed, although their awfulness did have one positive outcome: it made Noel want to join Oasis and be their light, their guide.

'You only get one chance, and it was staring me in the face,' he says. 'I told our kid the band were shite, but that he definitely had something as a frontman. Then I said, You either let me write the songs and we go for superstardom or else you stay here in Manchester all your lives like sad cunts.'

Talk about making them an offer they couldn't refuse! The band opted to let Noel take control of the operation, happy to leave all songwriting (and, later, arranging and producing) duties to their new mastermind. At last, Noel had an outlet for the songs he'd been writing in his spare time on days off and during Inspirals soundchecks.

Not that Noel was about to give up his increasingly frustrating day job – yet.

'The worst thing was knowing that I was miles better than the Inspirals were – miles better,' he looks back now. 'But I needed the money and that's why I stuck it out, cos getting a band off the ground is difficult. Not that that really mattered. I knew I was going to make it, whatever – I was born to do this.'

Invigorated by his new-found sense of conviction, Noel bought Oasis' equipment and the band started rehearsing in a room under the Boardwalk. He also realised he had to give up his roadie work to concentrate on Oasis and help perfect the band's sound.

Noel's decision to go all-out with Oasis also enabled them to play the occasional local pub gig, which they did, to the disinterest of all and sundry.

★★★★★★★★★★★★★★★★★★★

'Supersonic'
'Give me gin and tonic'

Oasis in Moseley, March 1994

18 Wheeler

TUT TUT

SOMETHING just had to happen, and soon. No band with this much total belief in their own sheer brilliance could fail to make at least some waves.

The opportunity to make a bigger splash arose completely by chance in May 1993, after over a year of rehearsing and refining the Oasis sound. Sister Lovers were an all-girl Manchester group named after early Seventies US cult band Big Star's celebrated third LP-cum-monument to misery. Oasis had befriended Sister Lovers and, when the latter scored a support slot at Glasgow's King Tut's Wah Wah Hut with the Big Star-influenced band, 18 Wheeler, they hitched a ride with them all the way up to Scotland.

Having travelled hundreds of miles, however, Oasis realised they wanted a little more payback for their effort than two hours' worth of audience-mingling with several hundred Glaswegians. No, what Oasis wanted was to do what they were convinced they were put on Earth to do: to play live. So badly did they want to perform, in fact, that, after being politely told to wise up and piss off by the club's promoter, they threatened material damage, physical violence and all manner of carnage and general chaotic unpleasantness. Oasis were grudgingly allowed to play a short four-song set. The story may well have ended there had fate not intervened for a second time in one night. Because who just happened to have turned up early that evening to catch the support act and was standing unexpectedly in the crowd when Oasis appeared to perform their impromptu four-song slot? None other than Creation Records boss, Alan McGee, there to see his new signings, 18 Wheeler.

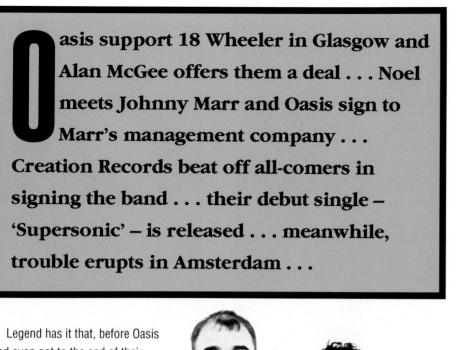

Oasis support 18 Wheeler in Glasgow and Alan McGee offers them a deal . . . Noel meets Johnny Marr and Oasis sign to Marr's management company . . . Creation Records beat off all-comers in signing the band . . . their debut single – 'Supersonic' – is released . . . meanwhile, trouble erupts in Amsterdam . . .

hailing Oasis as not only 'like The Jesus And Mary Chain if they'd been able to play their instruments' but also (albeit a hackned claim) 'the future of rock'n'roll'.

Then McGee allegedly surpassed himself for sheer unbridled, spontaneous lunacy when he jumped onstage and, cheque-book in hand, offered the band a five-album contract on the spot.

'He came up to us and went, "Have youse got a record deal, man?"' recalls Noel. 'And we went, "No." And he went, "D'youse want one?"'

Legend has it that, before Oasis had even got to the end of their first number, McGee had poured half a bottle of Jack Daniel's over his head and was seen melodramatically clutching his heart, proclaiming Liam Gallagher to be the magical mix of John Lydon and John Lennon he'd been waiting for since the dawn of Creation, and

Guigsy . . .

. . . Bonehead . . .

. . . and, um, Noely ?

MOVING ON UP

SO, after that bizarrely fortuitous four-song set – only their 20th gig thus far – Oasis were set to be part of what they considered to be 'the greatest rock'n'roll label in the world', the former resting place of leftfield renegades The Jesus And Mary Chain and innovative sound-weavers My Bloody Valentine as well as the current home of Primal Scream, Ride, Sugar and Teenage Fanclub (mind you, when the time came to sign on the dotted line in winter 1993, rumour has it that Noel would only put pen to paper if and when Creation did something about labelmates Slowdive, Swervedriver and Shonen Knife, who, reckoned Gallagher, were 'the biggest pile of shite I've ever heard in my life!').

Not that Alan McGee regretted his rash behaviour that night at King Tut's. And the indie majordomo was even more convinced when he received Oasis' demo cassette.

The cover of the tape was striking enough, featuring the band's now-familiar twisted Union Jack logo. And the music was nothing short of spellbinding. Included on the cassette (which is impossible to find nowadays, due to the fact that only about ten copies were made) are early versions of

'Fade Away', 'Married With Children', 'Columbia', 'Digsy's Dinner', 'I Will Believe', 'Alive', 'D'Yer Wanna Be A Spaceman?' and 'Bring It On Down'.

A few days after hearing the tape, Noel, Liam and Bonehead came down to meet the Creation posse in North London. But it was in their home base Manchester that Oasis got lucky for the third time in their short career. Noel had a chance encounter with a bloke he'd known from the Hacienda club simply as Ian, who happened to ask Gallagher for a copy of their demo so he could play it to his younger brother.

Ian's younger brother turned out to be Noel's hero from The Smiths, Johnny Marr! Marr heard the tape, came to see Oasis play at Manchester's Hop & Grapes, Marr told Marcus Russell (of Electronic's management company, Ignition) about this great new band he'd heard and Russell, after seeing them support Dodgy, offered to work for Oasis. (Equally exciting for Noel was that Marr gave him the guitar he used on The Smiths' best album, 'The Queen Is Dead', a Gibson Les Paul once owned by The Who's Pete Townshend!)

The cumulative effect of all this record company and management interest – not

forgetting the all-important first two reviews in the weekly music press, the *NME* review of their August gig at the Boardwalk celebrating the band's 'brilliant melodic framework', and the *Melody Maker* review (their first 'lead review', with a photo of Liam) of their September performance at the 'In The City' festival homing in on their 'exuberant, menacing freshness' and 'shimmery, rich sound' – was, simply, a bidding war of quite unrivalled ferocity. At one point, U2's Mother label allegedly promised to double any of the twenty or more other offers on the table.

Finally, on October 22nd 1993, Creation became the envy of every record label in Britain when Oasis signed to the label in the UK, with Sony picking up the rights for the rest of the world. There was just one problem to overcome before Noel put pen to paper, however – there were photos of Oasis' most hated band, quintessential baggy thug-rockers The Farm, on the wall at Creation HQ and they just had to go.

'I was like, I'm sorry, but we don't sign unless that picture's removed,' says Noel. 'They didn't take me seriously until I said: Look, I'm going to the toilet and I ain't coming out till it's gone. The Farm just rub us up the wrong way. They're chancers, but they think they're The Beatles.'

The band celebrated their signing, and the removal of the Farm snap, by entering what they now affectionately refer to as their 'Hamburg Period', hawking their wares around every toilet-venue in the land, supporting the likes of Verve, Liz Phair, The Milltown Brothers, St Etienne, The Real People and, as they put it, 'countless other shit bands'. The paying public generally remained indifferent to Creation's hot new signing, an indifference which helped the band hone to perfection a very useful 'no one likes us and we don't care' attitude.

Extremely useful, in fact, because, before the band had even reached stage one of their career – the debut single – the *NME* had tried to start the Oasis backlash, a live review of their Birmingham Institute gig in December describing Liam Gallagher as a 'vaguely Ian Brown-as-Tim Burgess slob of a frontman, singing in a vaguely tuneless half-whine, vaguely shaking a tambourine'. Liam later told another *NME* hack that if he ever met the reviewer in question, he would 'fuckin' slap the dick all around'.

That same week, however, *Melody Maker* rectified matters when journalist Calvin Bush gushed thus: 'They play eight songs, seven of which are more marvellous than Lena Olin in slinky black lingerie and a bowler hat. They are, frankly, incredible. They leave. I gasp and ache. The thought of having to wait a whole 10 days until they play here again is cramping my (life)style.'

I guess he liked them.

Naturally, there was far higher hyperbole to come . . .

'DAM BUSTERS

OASIS spent the first couple of months of 1994 in a variety of recording studios, attempting to get together enough tracks to be able to release a new single every two or three months a la The Beatles and the Stones, as well as enough for an album. The band zigzagged from Liverpool's Pink Museum, where they wrote what was to be their debut single 'Supersonic' in a mere

Liam gives it loads of frontman arrogance, September '93

Oasis hit the Midlands, March '94

Oasis' very own Buddy Rich, Tony McCarroll

eight hours, to Monmouth's £800-a-day Monnow Studios (where they just managed to run through a few ramshackle Rolling Stones covers with Noel on vocals), to the famous Olympic Studios in Barnes, to Cornwall's Sawmills Studios, to Manchester's Out Of The Blue, to Wales' Loco Studios, to London's Matrix.

And yet, in spite of all this gadding about, and apart from the 'Supersonic' sessions, hardly anything had been committed to vinyl – we were yet to hear Oasis on record. That said, in December 1993, those teasers at Creation did whet our appetites when they sent out to various press and radio types a white label promotional 12-inch of 'Columbia' from the band's demo tape. Radio 1FM took one listen to this raw mix of an already rough and ragged track and playlisted it, the first time they had ever done so with an unreleased song.

So we were at least getting some idea of what Oasis would sound like. In January 1994, 200 people had to be turned away from the band's debut appearance in the capital at the Water Rats in King's Cross, although the lucky few hundred who managed to do sardine impressions got to see what Liam, Noel, Guigs, Bonehead and Tony looked like.

And then, in February 1994, the third part of the puzzle started to fall into place when we got an opportunity to find out what Oasis were really like as people. There had already been reports of furious band in-fighting and fraternal imbroglios on the road with Whiteout earlier in the year, suggesting Oasis were the latest in a long line of hooligan rockers from the Stones to The Sex

A rare glimpse of Oasis smiling. Sort of.

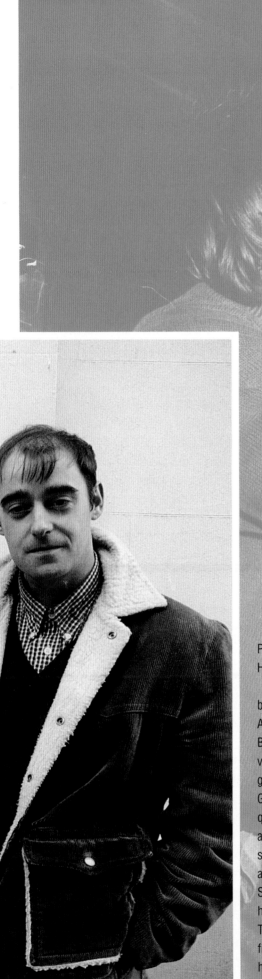

Pistols to Frankie Goes To Hollywood to Happy Mondays.

But it was on February 18th, when the band were scheduled to support Verve in Amsterdam for their first ever gig outside Britain, that we got our first truly explicit view of The Real Oasis. Apparently, only Noel got off the ferry from Harwich. Liam and Guigs had reputedly got drunk on enormous quantities of champagne and Jack Daniel's and became involved in scuffles with security men and police, generally brawling and smashing up furniture along the way. Stated the *NME*: 'The pair were then handcuffed and locked in the brig.' The following morning, Bonehead awoke to find that his room had been ransacked and his passport and clothes stolen. He was also apprehended by the authorities for causing a disturbance along with Tony McCarroll after

loudly banging on the doors of numerous neighbouring cabins. Consequently, the four band members were placed in a dockyard cell upon the ferry's arrival in Holland, and then promptly deported by the local authorities. Poor old Noel was forced to make his way to the venue on his own and call off the gig.

Liam thought the whole incident was pretty funny and very rock'n'roll. Noel begged to differ.

'Nah, rock'n'roll is playing in Amsterdam, coming back, and telling everyone you blew 'em away,' he said. 'NOT getting thrown off the ferry like some scouse schlepper with handcuffs. That's just football hooliganism.'

'SONIC' BOOM

BEFORE their reputation for rucking could overshadow their reputation for, um,

Oasis storm *The Word*

rock'n'rolling, Oasis released their riotous first single 'Supersonic' in April 1994.

We had already been blown away by a live performance of the song on *The Word*, their TV debut, in March. Now we could bring the raw energy of this ravishingly exciting young band into our homes whenever we wanted with the band's new four-track Creation EP.

'Supersonic' itself was based around such a naggingly infectious chord sequence it was like you'd heard it before many times, and yet. already. it felt as much like Oasis as anything else. A simple celebration of hedonism and epic audacity ('Feeling supersonic/Give me gin and tonic' drawled Liam, easily the cockiest singer since Ian Brown), the words also offered a glimpse into Noel Gallagher's psychedelic imagination ('I know a girl called Elsa/She's into Alka Seltzer/She sniffs it through a cane on a supersonic train . . . she done it with a doctor on a helicopter'), pure John Lennon-circa-'I Am The Walrus'-meets-Shaun Ryder-esque lysergic whimsy.

Noel had a succinct explanation of the song's lyrics: 'It's just about some fucking nine-stone geezer who got Charlie'd off his nut one night.'

Of the extra tracks, 'Take Me Away' was a melancholy acoustic number sung by Noel with echoes of Harry Nillson's plaintive 'Everybody's Talkin'' (from the film *Midnight Cowboy*), 'I Will Believe' was a simple live rocker and 'Columbia' was the white label demo recording.

From the sleeve of the single – a wide angle shot of the band tuning up in the studio surrounded by guitars, amps and assorted equipment – to the music itself, it was clear from the off that Oasis were about Classic Rock'N'Roll, all cocky postures, delinquent braggadocio, insouciance that verged on arrogance, simply brutal (boorish?) rifferama and an almost Luddite aversion to the technological advances of the late 20th century.

The public didn't hesitate to demonstrate their own love of classic rock'n'roll when they sent 'Supersonic' soaring to Number 31 in the charts.

★★★★☆☆☆☆☆☆☆★★★★

'Shakermaker'
'It's the right time'

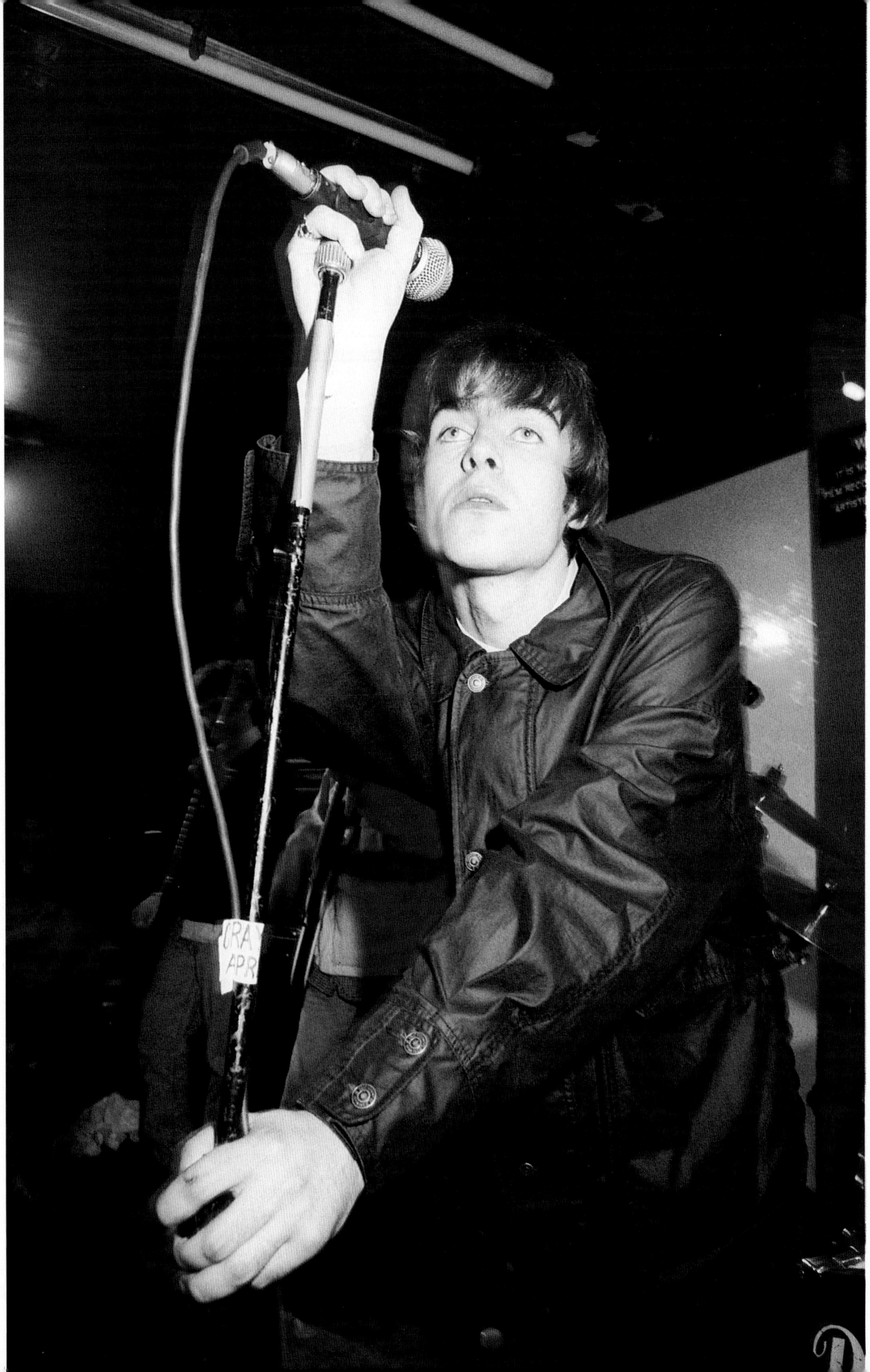

The brothers Gallagher seal their group's reputation as The Most Argumentative Band in Britain . . . second single 'Shakermaker' nearly gets the band sued by Coca-Cola . . . Oasis get to Number 11! . . . and appear on Top Of The Pops . . .

Noel Gallagher, heir to Johnny Marr's throne ?

BROTHERS IN QUALMS

IT was in April that Oasis really cemented their dual reputations as The Best New Band In Britain – with 'Supersonic' as well as a series of ferocious live shows, notably their incendiary performance at the 100 Club in London's Oxford Street – and The Most Argumentative New Band In Britain.

It was their first major feature, in the *NME*, that brought to the nation's attention the extent of the damage these headstrong young brothers were prepared to do to each other. There was even a photo alongside the piece that showed Liam trying to take a swing at Noel.

Then there was the text . . .

First, there were the dazzlingly daft non-sequiturs:

Liam: 'You want to be Andrew Lloyd Webber, you do. You fucker.'

Noel: 'Who's Andrew Lloyd Webber?'

Liam: 'I haven't got a clue. He's a golfer, or something . . . I'm just an average lad who was born in Burnage, who played conkers.'

Noel: 'CONKERS?'

Liam: 'Conkers, mate. Conkers. The fucking lot. Conkers. That is it.'

Oasis at legendary haunt, the 100 Club

Then there was the heated exchange about the negative review of Oasis live the previous December by NME stringer, Johnny Cigarettes:

Liam: 'I'll slap him [Cigarettes] around the show.'

Noel: 'Shut up, man. SHUT UP!'

Liam: 'No, you shut up.'

Noel: 'No, YOU shut up.'

Liam: 'No, you shut up. If I ever meet the fucker, I'll slap him.'

Noel: 'You're talking shit.'

Liam: 'I'll hit him with a bottle, right in his kipper. I'll smash the fuck right out of him.'

Their future's so bright, they gotta wear . . .

Then things really got nasty:

'Let's fucking go, then, you DICK! Let's have a fucking FIGHT!' yelled Liam, offering to place a good, hard punch in his elder sibling's face as the journalist and press officer took an embarrassed back seat.

'I hate this bastard,' Liam ranted on, to no one in particular, pointing in the direction of Noel. 'And that's what it's all about. That's why we'll be the best band in the world, cos I fucking hate that twat there. And I hope one day there's a time when I can smash the fuck out of him. With a fucking Rickenbacker. Right on his nose. And then he can do the same to me.'

'How often do we argue?' Liam repeated the hack's question. 'Every day. Hourly. But it's not hate. It's love. I don't hate him. It's love. It's one of them. We're brothers, man. It's deep shit.'

Liam may have put down their frequent and furious bust-ups – which smacked (literally!) of the scraps 30 years previous between Ray and Dave Davies of The Kinks – to subconscious brotherly love, but, in an interview with *Loaded*, the Bible Of Lad, Noel had a different slant on matters fraternal.

'If I lived in America, I would have blown his [Liam's] head off by now and completely regretted it,' he was quoted in the macho mag. 'Since I live in England, though, I just give him a black eye or something every now and again. I don't hate him, but fuck me he pisses me off sometimes.

'Thing is,' Noel put forward his theory, 'Liam don't write no lyrics, he doesn't play any instrument, doesn't write nothing – so all he's required to do is stand there and sing and fucking look good. And I think he gets pissed off by the fact that he doesn't actually do anything because he can't. I dunno, I think he just winds me up on purpose, the cunt. I think it's just boredom. I don't know what to do. We can't even agree to disagree.'

Noel put it simplest in the style magazine *The Face*: 'He's a genius frontman and was born to do this. But he also wishes he was me. Always has done.'

Oasis were also shaping up as possibly the most ambitous, audacious and arrogant

Liam shakes his maker at New Cross, May '94

Oasis: so hard, they'll rob your hub-caps

The 'increasingly lunatic' Guigsy

new band in Britain – and that's just the 'A's – who rarely (if ever) let an occasion go by without making an outragous assertion about the band's brilliance and/or inevitable superstar status.

'We're the musical equivalent of Muhammad Ali,' they said in *The European*. 'I think we'll be the most important band in the world. We'll be the new Beatles,' the band informed the *NME*. 'We're the best band on the planet. That's not arrogance, that's just a fact,' they boasted in *Smash Hits*. 'Us and [Paul] Weller are the only real class on this bill,' they said of the Glastonbury 1994 line-up. 'I pity anyone who doesn't buy our records,' they told *Melody Maker*, adding that 'even The Stone Roses couldn't write a song like "Supersonic".'

And, as early as August, they were telling *Select* magazine that they would be Number One by Christmas '94 with the still-unrecorded 'Whatever'.

Thing is, most of their assertions weren't really all that outrageous when you thought about it – they were true.

Well, sort of, anyway.

COKE ADDICTS

OASIS, it was quickly becoming clear, were not afraid of anything, least of all controversy. Which was just as well, because they were attracting plenty of it.

Oasis know what time it is – literally!

They were teetering especially close to the edge with 'Shakermaker', their second single, released in June '94, due to its uncanny melodic resemblance to the ancient Coca-Cola jingle, the one sung by The New Seekers and used by the huge multi-national conglomerate as their early Seventies advertising campaign theme, 'I'd Like To Teach The World To Sing'. It was so similar, in fact, that Creation actually feared that the all-powerful Coca-Cola Corporation might consider suing them.

For quite a while, Oasis had actually appropriated the line, 'I'd like to buy the world a Coke', for live renditions of 'Shakermaker', and now the band's songwriter Noel Gallagher wanted to keep it on the recorded version. As far as he was concerned, there was no way the line was going to be cut out.

'We might have to write off half the royalties, but fuck it!' he said at the time. 'For someone in a suit to come along and say we've got to change a song we've been playing for two years isn't on.'

However, when 'Shakermaker' came out, it didn't feature the line, even if the tune itself was still uncomfortably similar to The New Seekers original, Liam howling 'I'd like to be somebody else and not know where I've been' so that it scanned to fit in with the original Coke theme.

Bonehead in yet another sumptuous gig location

Not that any of this mattered much, as 'Shakermaker' remains easily Oasis' weakest single to date, and no amount of petty musical larceny could hide the fact that this was a song in search of a decent chord progression, a hackneyed riff only brightened up by daft lyrical references to various characters such as Mr Soft, Mr Clean and Mr Ben who, according to the first verse, were living in Noel's loft. Or something.

As for the extra tracks, 'D'Yer Wanna be A Spaceman?' was a wafer-thin slice of acoustic whimsy, 'Alive' (an 8-track demo) was another crude rocker, while 'Bring It On Down' was a live version of a blistering song that sounded tinny and tame after translation onto vinyl/CD.

And yet, such was the force of the hype machine by this point in the Oasis saga that 'Shakermaker' couldn't fail to crashland into the upper reaches of the charts, which it did, entering in its first week at Number 11. That meant two-out-of-two hits so far.

It also meant Oasis could make their debut appearance on *Top Of The Pops*, a performance which certainly made up for the relatively disappointing music and which, for sheer alien delinquent cheek, almost ranked alongside Nirvana's *TOTP* appearance for 'Smells Like Teen Spirit', The Smiths for 'This Charming Man' and The Associates for 'Party Fears Two'.

The single's success chart-wise was undoubtedly helped by a ludicrously effusive Single Of The Week review in *Melody Maker* by Paul Mathur that described 'Shakermaker' as 'one of the hundred greatest songs ever written'.

As I say, ludicrous.

Oasis in Liverpool, April 1994

★★★★★★☆☆☆☆★★★★★★

'Live Forever'

'I just want to fly'

The Face rechristens the band 'The Sex Beatles' as Oasismania sweeps Britain . . . Oasis play their first festival – Glastonbury . . . Noel jams with Crazy Horse . . . and more bad boy behaviour at the Columbia hotel . . . Oasis hit America's New Music Seminar

SUMMER MADNESS

OASIS kept themselves busy during the first few months of summer '94, playing live, appearing at various festivals, jet-setting, being interviewed by every magazine under and over the sun (style Bible *The Face* put Oasis on the cover with the line: 'Never Mind The Bollocks, Here's The Sex Beatles'!!), and generally maintaining their reputation as pop's latest angels with dirty faces, getting into and out of more scrapes than most bands manage in a lifetime.

Oasis went on their first, sell-out headline tour in May, while Noel and Bonehead performed at 'Undrugged', Creation Records' 10th anniversary concert at the Royal Albert Hall, playing the band's forthcoming single 'Live Forever' as well as a primitive early version of 'Whatever'.

Then, in June, they made their festival debut at Glastonbury.

'Are you gonna wake up, then, for some real songs?' Liam goaded the sun-kissed, zonked-out, crusty student masses upon taking the stage. The band stormed through nine songs, including an encore of 'I Am The Walrus', to an ecstatic reaction. Excerpts from their festival performance were shown on Channel 4's *4 Goes To Glastonbury*.

Oasis', or at least Noel's, peak live moment surely came three days earlier, however, when he joined the ex-Icicle Works (the Liverpool band who had a hit 10 years before with 'Love Is A Wonderful Colour') frontman Ian McNabb onstage at London's King's College. McNabb was playing that night with Ralph Molina and Billy Talbot of Crazy Horse, the legendary cohorts of grizzly old rocker Neil Young.

Noel, a huge fan of Young and Crazy Horse, leapt at the chance to play alongside his heroes, and the foursome proceeded to rampage through a rousing version of 'Pushin' Too Hard' by original Sixties punks Sky Saxon And The Seeds, as well as a snatch of 'Rescue' by post-punk Liverpudlians Echo & The Bunnymen. (The brief King's College set was taped, and may well be issued at some point in 1995.) Crazy Horse themselves were so impressed with

Oasis wake up the blissed-out hordes, Glastonbury '94

Oasis unplugged at 'Undrugged', June 1994

Gallagher's impromptu jamming abilities that they travelled all the way to Manchester to see Oasis play live a few days later.

A euphoric Noel beamed, 'My mum's dead proud of me. I've had my picture taken with Arthur Lee [of Love], I've been onstage with Crazy Horse and I'm going to have my picture taken with Johnny Cash. All I need now is my picture taken with Burt Bacharach and I've got the full set!'

On a more serious note, he said of his jam with Crazy Horse: 'We're already respected by bands from the Sixties. We're respected by Paul Weller. You won't see Thom from fucking Radiohead playing with the Velvet fucking Underground or whatever.'

All of this furious activity must have gone to Noel and co's heads, because the night after Glastonbury the band got into a whole heap of mischief at legendary rock'n'roll hotel, the Columbia, in West London. By the band's own account, they got seriously drunk and, to cut a long story short, 'Things went out windows . . . we trashed the place.'

Elaborated Liam: 'They put us in the Columbia and at first it was a buzz being there. But then I thought it was a dive. There was a bug in the corner of my room and I thought, You can fuck off, this is my room. We had enough in the end. There was a lot of pot going round and we'd got some pipes. We were drinking as well and in the end we just trashed it. Then we started running round the place and going for it.'

The Columbia reacted by doing what they had only done twice before in their illustrious rock'n'roll history, to The Fall and The Mission: they banned Oasis.

The *Guardian* newspaper, obviously feeling this to be a high (or rather low) point in the celebrated history of rock'n'roll uncivil disobedience, an epoch-making incident on a par with The Rolling Stones urinating against a garage wall and The Beatles spliffing up in the bogs of Buckingham Palace after getting their OBEs, ran a two-pager detailing three decades of bad r'n'r behaviour in response to Oasis' laddish antics, antics which apparently involved – merciful heavens! – throwing their shoes around the hotel bar.

Oasis themselves were unrepentant. Said the Mancunian miscreants afterwards: 'Fuck 'em, we don't care. There's better hotels. It was the sort of place your Gran would have stayed in anyway.'

FOREVER PEOPLE

AT the end of July, Oasis played Tennants' 'T In the Park' Festival in Strathyclyde's Country Park, before heading off to Sweden to play the Hultsfred Festival.

High spirited as per usual, and assisted this time by their equally lively festival-mates Primal Scream and Verve (the latter are one of the few contemporary British groups whose music Oasis actually like), Oasis made front page news in the national press with some by-now-obligatory on-the-road shenanigans involving the smashing up of yet another hotel bar.

Backstage at Glastonbury

Let's raise one for America, July '94

'Hello, Room Trashing Incorporated – can I help you?'

Oasis: re-born in the USA

Liam recalls the event: 'I was walking along and this chair came flying past me. Then another, then another. I thought, It's gonna be good tonight. Primal Scream took off because we were getting a bit rowdy. They booked out at about two in the morning after we'd just smashed the place up – ripped the phones out and threw 'em out the window. We got arrested and banned from Sweden, and Primal Scream got off, the cunts.' Both Oasis and Verve were forced to pay nearly £1,000 in damages to the manager of the hotel, and, contrary to Liam's account, just managed to escape arrest after the police were called. To add injury to insult, Liam broke his foot while jumping off the tour bus the next day.

Before that little lot went off, though, Oasis had continent-hopped all the way to the States along with the cream of 1994's Britpack – Echobelly, These Animal Men, S*M*A*S*H, The Orb and Kaliphz – to play New York's annual industry round-up of new talent, the New Music Seminar.

The band were shadowed every step of the way by *Melody Maker*'s intrepid Paul Mathur. First he accompanied them to their American debut at Wetlands on 21st July (where they were sandwiched between Lotion and X-CNN), a performance subsequently described by Mathur in the paper as 'one of the best sets I've ever seen them play, Liam's [Johnny] Rottenesque sneer honed to perfection, Noel sublimely transcendent on guitar, the band just KNOWING they've got it exactly right.'

Mathur also listened in as the band blabbed their way through as many exclamatory claims ('We never, ever had any doubt that all of this would happen'; 'We're more important than some stupid industry circus') and defamatory put-downs (Liam on the shotgun suicide of Kurt Cobain: 'Don't talk to me about Nirvana. He was just a sad cunt who couldn't handle the fame. We're stronger than that. And you can fuck your fucking Pearl Jam as well') as they could squeeze into seven days.

Oasis tune up, Stateside

Finally, the 'Maker journalist watched as the band filmed the video for their next single, 'Live Forever', in New York's Central Park. Liam really wanted to make the most of the opportunity and turn the event into an impromptu open-air gig by hiring a PA, but Noel flatly refused.

'Elvis Presley doesn't want to do it,' whinged Liam about his elder brother in a now familiar display of fraternal animosity. 'That's why he's a cunt and I hate him.'

There may have been no last-minute concert for the benefit of the tramps who roam Manhattan's most famous bit of greenery, but the video did get made in time for the release of the third Oasis single on August 8th, the week Melody Maker and NME broke tradition and both put the band on the front cover (it was, in fact, the first time the two 'inkies' had featured the same cover stars since U2 broke their silence in 1988 – apart from news coverage of the death of Kurt Cobain, of course) and 25 years to the day since The Beatles' renowned 'Abbey Road' zebra crossing LP shoot. The latter may or may not explain why the sleeve of 'Live Forever' featured a photo of the house where John Lennon grew up.

Like their first two singles, 'Live Forever' was backed with an acoustic number ('Up In The Sky', later electrified for the 'Definitely Maybe' album) and live track ('Supersonic', recorded in concert in April '94), as well as a song called 'Cloudburst', a hard'n'heavy chunk of psychedelic rock.

On their own, these three tracks would have made for a reasonably rewarding EP. However, 'Live Forever', of all the Oasis singles to date, was the one that least required any additives. A soaring anthem with a majestic chord progression courtesy of Noel and a deliciously plaintive vocal performance from Liam, 'Live Forever' is a glorious celebration of the potency of positive thinking and the absolute,

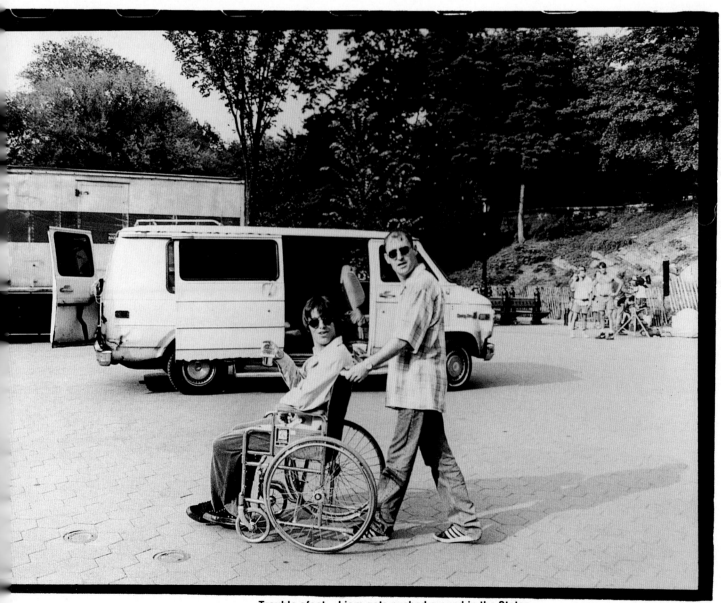

Trouble afoot – Liam gets pushed around in the States

unadulterated feeling of total possibility that is the natural right of the very beautiful and the very young.

'Live Forever' remains one of the best singles to be released this decade and was, along with Blur's 'Girls & Boys', by far the finest single of 1994. It was the record that cut the crap, the one that finally proved Oasis were more than just Manc motormouths with a cabal of overenthusiastic supporters in the media and an overweening sense of their own importance. Moreover, it was the record that suggested that here was a band destined for at least some of the greatness they believed to be their birthright.

As Noel told the *Melody Maker*, 'There's more to us than rumours, hearsay, gossip and sensationalism about drugs and fucking shagging in hotel rooms. This is what we're all about – songs. We're a real band with real songs and everything else is just incidental. That's what we'll be remembered for in 20 years' time, not incidents on ferries or drug busts or whatever.'

'Live Forever' was, basically, a classic. And it got to Number 10; Number One would have been about right.

★★★★★✰✰✰✰✰✰✰✰★★

'Definitely Maybe'

'Give it all you've got'

Oasis' 'Definitely Maybe' enters the British album charts at Number One . . . beating the popular operatics of the Three Tenors, it becomes the fastest selling debut LP of all time . . . Evan Dando of The Lemonheads jams with the marvels from Manchester at Virgin Records, Marble Arch . . .

RECORD BREAKERS

EVEN after scrapping entire sessions and using as many as seven – count 'em – studios, Oasis' debut album 'Definitely Maybe' still only cost a very modest £75,000. It was eventually produced by Noel Gallagher's mate from his Inspirals days, Mark Coyle, and Noel himself, while Electronic's producer Owen Morris was responsible for additional production, mastering and mixing chores.

Thanks to a colossal amount of pre-release press and the sort of buzz the industry definitely hadn't heard since the week before Suede's debut LP came out in 1993, maybe even since the release of the first Frankie Goes To Hollywood album in 1984, advance orders for 'Definitely Maybe' reached an unprecedented level.

As for the week it actually came out, there were yet more records broken. 'Definitely Maybe' first hit the shops on Tuesday August 30th (records are normally released on a

Liam and Noel plus friend (Evan Dando!) at Virgin Marble Arch

Monday, but that week it was a Bank Holiday). Within a few days, it had apparently sold about 150,000 copies, making it the fastest-selling debut album of the Nineties, as well as, arguably, the biggest-selling debut album of all time.

Needless to say, it entered the album charts at Number One, one place ahead of 'The Three Tenors' LP by globally famous

opera singers José Carreras, Placido Domingo and Luciano Pavarotti, a record which had been expected to sail to pole position given their huge across-the-board popularity as well as a television advertising campaign costing an estimated £2 million. Some reports stated that 'Definitely Maybe' actually sold between 10 and 20,000 more copies in its first week of release than 'The Three Tenors'. A spokesman for Creation Records – who, after ten years' releasing singles and albums, were now enjoying their very first Number One in any chart (they came very close with Primal Scream's 'Give Out But Don't Give Up' LP, which reached Number Two, and Sugar's 'Beaster' album [at Number Three]) – wryly commented: 'Three fat blokes shouting are no competition for Oasis.'

As for Oasis themselves, a spokesman for the band said: 'They love it. They say, "We're mad for it." They want to be the biggest band. There's no point settling for anything less. You've gotta have ambition.'

The very same day 'Definitely Maybe' was released, 1,000 Oasis fans turned up at the Marble Arch branch of Virgin Megastore to see their favourite band perform an impromptu acoustic, *Unplugged*-style selection of tracks from the album. Unfortunately, although Virgin have an entertainments licence from Westminster City Council, they are limited to a 200 capacity, so, when the band started playing, only a small number of their devotees were allowed in to watch.

Eventually, Oasis ran through their three hit singles, as well as 'Sad Song' (an extra track only available on the vinyl version of the album) and 'Slide Away'.

And then, as they prepared to play future Christmas smash 'Whatever', they were joined by Sultan of Slacker, Evan Dando of The Lemonheads, who proceeded to rattle a tambourine and add backing vocals to the song! After the brief show, Dando explained to *Melody Maker* how he had become Noel

Gallagher's mate as well as Oasis' biggest fan.

'We met about a month ago and hit it off,' said the flaxen-haired indie pin-up. 'Then, last night, we collided in Paris. We'd both been playing the Lowlands festival in Holland and we wrote a song together called "Purple Parallelogram".

'I really like Oasis' lack of pretension,' he added, 'but I won't be signing any autographs today because that would be impolite. This is their day.'

Indeed it was.

'Definitely Maybe' has subsequently sold almost half-a-million copies in the UK – making it a platinum album – as well as thousands more overseas.

Not bad for a first shot.

CERTAINLY . . . PROBABLY

BUT was it any good?

Definitely! Maybe . . .

One couldn't help but have at least some reservations about the band's debut album. First of all, on a purely value-for-money basis, there were only five tracks diehard Oasis fans wouldn't have owned before (and they would probably have heard those live) – 'Rock'N'Roll Star', 'Cigarettes & Alcohol' (which was due to be the band's fourth single anyway), 'Digsy's Dinner', 'Slide Away' and 'Married With Children' – or six if you happened to buy the vinyl version of 'Definitely Maybe', because it contained the previously unavailable 'Sad Song'.

And secondly, notwithstanding the excellence of much of the material, there was a definite whiff of déja vu about the whole project due in no small part to Oasis' stubborn insistence on the conventional four-square rock band line-up of guitar, bass, drums and vocals. Suffice it to say that none of the tracks would have jarred had they been aired in '84, '74 or, indeed, 1964.

Not only that, but you would have been hard pressed to squeeze all the obvious steals and examples of creative pilfering into a three-volume book. You didn't need to be an anorak-clad obsessive with an encyclopaedic knowledge of rock history to spot all the T-Rex, Sex Pistols, Stone Roses,

Beatles, Rolling Stones, Happy Mondays, Kinks, David Bowie, Small Faces, Faces, Neil Young, Jam and Who musical references liberally sprinkled all over the (mainly CD) 'grooves' of 'Definitely Maybe'.

In fact, some tracks were virtually replicas of ancient material. 'Digsy's Dinner', to cite one example, had such a similar riff to 'Lazy Sunday' by The Small Faces it was a surprise writs weren't issued within days of 'Definitely Maybe' coming out. And 'Cigarettes & Alcohol' was so like T-Rex's 'Get It On', it's a wonder poor old Marc Bolan hasn't dug his way out of his Bushey grave to wreak posthumous revenge on the outrageously cheeky Noel Gallagher.

But perhaps all this was missing the point somewhat. Because, as I myself pointed out in my review of the album in the August 27th issue of *Melody Maker*, 'You shouldn't expect samples, sequencers, dance beats or

any other concessions to late-20th century pop life here. Nor should you anticipate any idiosyncratic curlicues or strange experiments in sound. Fuck that – that's what The Prodigy, Orbital and The Aphex Twin are for. Oasis have been called retro – you can fuck that as well.

'In no other sphere of human activity than pop music,' I ranted on (and on), 'do we apply such rigorous attention to originality of intent or achievement. Do we turn off 'The Bill' because it's not as good as 'The Sweeney'? Do we chuck out our dinner because it doesn't taste as good as something we ate back in the Eighties?! Do we fuck - no, we surrender to the gloriously vivid immediacy of the moment.'

BACK-TRACKING

THE above attitude certainly helped overcome any misgivings I, or anyone else

for that matter, may have had about the sometimes absurdly familiar nature of Oasis' trad-rock attack.

Besides, once you'd managed to get over the LP material's lack of originality, you were free to enjoy what was nearly one hour's worth of good, old-fashioned, brash, electric, energetic rock'n'roll. If nothing else, like 'Suede' (in hock to David Bowie up to its elbows), 'The Stone Roses' (ditto, only for Bowie read The Byrds) and Teenage Fanclub's 'Bandwagonesque' (Big Star) before it, 'Definitely Maybe' proves that, as far as rock'n'roll is concerned, the future may well be just a tad overrated.

Or, as Paul Mathur beautifully put it, 'Eleven tracks, each a potential single, and the whole a fully-formed, power chord-drenched justification for why guitar music can rape the senses.'

Exactly.

Oasis rock the Astoria, August '94

As an LP-opener, 'Rock'N'Roll Star' was fantastically exciting, an inspiring paean to the power of the imagination and arguably the most explosive introduction to any album since 'The Headmaster Ritual' kickstarted The Smiths' 'Meat Is Murder'. 'Shakermaker' and 'Live Forever', the next two songs, were untouched in their transition from single to album. 'Up In The Sky' was a ferociously amped-up version of the track that originally appeared on the B-side of the 'Live Forever' single. 'Columbia' was as wild, wired and weird as ever, a terrace chant in search of a football match.

Then came 'Supersonic', as snottily infectious as ever ('You can have it all but how much do you want it?'). 'Bring It Down' was a raw guitar rampage worthy of the Pistols or The Stooges that managed to sound even more live than the live version previously available on the flip of 'Shakermaker'. 'Cigarettes & Alcohol' was another example of Noel Gallagher's genius for writing obscenely simple three-chord wonders that, after one play, you feel like

you've heard a zillion times – the mark of a great pop songwriter, that.

'Cigarettes & Alcohol' also demonstrated once more Noel's knack for coming up with naggingly memorable lyrics-cum-catchphrases ('You gotta make it happen!') as well as sneaky drug references ('You might as well do the white line'). If that wasn't enough, the track featured some superbly sneery Johnny Rottenish vowel/consonant extensions from brother Liam ('Is it myyyy imaginayyy-sheee-yunnn?') After that, 'Digsy's Dinner' was, as I've said, just a throwaway little jaunt down memory lane, one marked 'Steve Marriot'.

The 10th track, called 'Slide Away', was something else entirely, however. Over a gorgeously melancholy series of minor chords and some exquisite guitar patterns reminiscent of Neil Young circa 'Cortez The Killer' or 'Like A Hurricane', Liam, clearly singing on Noel's behalf (the latter split with his longterm girlfriend in 1994), mourned the loss of the love of his life ('I dream of you, and all the things you say/I wonder

where you are now . . .') while at the same time imagining the prospect of escaping dull reality with either the same, or another, girl of his fantasies ('Slide in, baby – together we'll fly'). Lovely.

After the orgasm, the anti-climax: 'Married With Children', a lighthearted acoustic anecdote (rock music should never, ever, be lighthearted), again obviously about Noel, and an ex-girlfriend who keeps moaning at him for playing crap music and keeping her awake at night with same. Very nice, in a Gerry & The Pacemakers sort of way. If you like that sort of thing.

'Sad Song' more than made up for 'Married With Children' (if you bought 'Definitely Maybe' on vinyl, that is), a gently pretty acoustic lament for lost love – yet again! – that suggested there was rather more to Noel Gallagher than just smashing up hotel bar furniture and defenestrating television sets.

As he told the NME's John Harris, 'I'm a lover, not a fighter.'

Hey!

Paul Weller's favourite new guitarist, Noel Gallagher

oasis

THE DEBUT GOLD ALBUM AVAILABLE ON ALL FORMATS OUT NOW

INCLUDES THE HITS: SUPERSONIC • SHAKERMAKER LIVE FOREVER • CIGARETTES & ALCOHOL

oasis Live

November
Wed 30 • Sout ~~SOLD OUT~~ a Guildhall

December
Thur 1 • Sheffi ~~SOLD OUT~~ gon
Sun 4 • Camb ~~SOLD OUT~~ rn Exchange
Wed 7 • Glasg ~~SOLD OUT~~ owlands
Thur 8 • Middl ~~SOLD OUT~~ gh Town Hall
Fri 9 • Liverp ~~SOLD OUT~~ l Court
Sun 11 • Wolv ~~SOLD OUT~~ on Civic Hall
Mon12 • Cardi ~~SOLD OUT~~ a
Wed 13 • Lond ~~SOLD OUT~~ mersmith Palais
Sun 18 • Man ~~SOLD OUT~~ Academy
Thur 29 • Brig ~~SOLD OUT~~ ntre

Oasis: better than Pavarotti, apparently

★★★★★★★★★★★★★★★★

'Cigarettes & Alcohol'
'You gotta make it happen!'

Top, Oasis hit Nagoya, Japan. Bottom, the fans in Dublin refuse to go home.

WHAT THE PAPERS SAID

THE reviews of 'Definitely Maybe' were almost universally ecstastic. Of the music weeklies, *NME* gave it an impressive 9/10 and said it was like 'opening your bedroom curtains one morning and discovering that some fucker's built the Taj Mahal in your back garden and then filled it with your favourite flavour of Angel Delight', which I'm sure meant something to the journalist when he wrote it; and *Melody Maker* called it 'a record full of songs to live by, made by a gang of reckless northern reprobates – yeah, we hacks love a bit of rough – who you can easily dream of joining.'

The monthlies were no less keen on the album. *Mojo* praised its 'spunky, adolescent rock'. *Q* called the album 'a riot . . . manna from heaven'. *Vox* correctly noted that Oasis 'have a faultless pedigree that includes every great British rock'n'roll band of the last 30

The album receives unanimously rave reviews in all sections of the press . . . despite it being the fourth single off the album, 'Cigarettes And Alcohol' gets to Number Seven . . . there is rising tension during the band's American tour, some shows being cancelled . . . and Noel Gallagher gets punched in Newcastle . . .

'Heil Oasis!' – Tokyo, September 1994

Noel jams with the Japanese Beatles

years'. And *Select*, awarding it five-out-of-five stars, decided that 'whatever The Stone Roses are doing out in Wales [the other great Manchester band of the last half decade or so had yet to release their long-awaited second album], they may as well pack up and go home'.

Even dance magazine *Mixmag*, who rarely if ever review guitar-based records, gave 'Definitely Maybe' 10/10 and concluded: 'If you're into music, be it techno, hip hop, jungle or classic hands-towards-the-ceiling pumping house, you could still get into this.'

Then there were the dailies – specifically the 'serious' broadsheets – normally less prone to dizzy hyperbole. The *Independent* commented: 'The UK can still be relied upon to throw up a classic world-beating guitar band every few years. Oasis are the best for some time.' The *Daily Telegraph* homed in on Oasis' 'jangly, swaggering pop songs and snappy, arrogant lyrics'. The *Guardian*

Noel and Liam: the brothers grim

The 'I Am The Walrus' sequence from the Beatles' *Magical Mystery Tour*

celebrated its 'guitar pop, distilled to its simplest, most infectious form, without ambiguity or gender confusion'. And *The Times* reckoned that, 'As an uncomplicated celebration of youthful brio, this is an album which takes some beating.'

In fact across the journalistic board, only David Cheal, offering a second opinion in the *Daily Telegraph*, had a less than kind word to say about Oasis at this point, making the comment: 'They have about as much chance of becoming the new Beatles as Dannii

Minogue has of becoming the new Diana Ross; they simply do not belong on the same musical planet, and catchy though songs like "Supersonic" and "Live Forever" may be, they are hardly likely to become ingrained in the very fabric of our culture . . .

'No,' he summed up, 'Oasis may not be the new Beatles, but with their gift for memorable hooks, their guitar-dominated sound and their penchant for meaningless lyrics, they could be the new Slade.' Bitch.

BEER WE GO AGAIN

THE general public clearly didn't give a fig about original this or Beatles that, because, when 'Cigarettes & Alcohol', the band's fourth single and the fourth to be lifted from 'Definitely Maybe', was released in October, it was bought by more people than any of their previous singles, entering the charts at a highly impressive Number Seven.

The success of 'Cigarettes & Alcohol' was doubly pleasing because it suggested that Oasis were doing what no other 'indie' band apart from Blur in recent years has done, and achieve that all-important crossover from critical faves to student raves to join that rare group reserved for the select few in the upper echelons of the Rock Stratosphere known simply as The People's Choice.

The sleeve of the single, with its carefully contrived shot of Oasis 'spontaneously' enjoying themselves and partying with various mates and girls and cigarettes and alcohol, indicated what we already suspected – that this was debauched and depraved business as usual.

Apart from the title track, the EP featured a ragged version of 'I Am The Walrus' recorded live in Glasgow in June '94, as well as the previously unreleased 'Listen Up' and 'Fade Away'. 'Listen Up' was arguably the best extra track yet offered free on their four EPs, a strident rock ballad with an affecting chord sequence all about how 'One fine day I'm gonna leave you all behind' (many of Noel Gallagher's lyrics are about escape to a better world – a rock star world?), while 'Fade Away' was a blistering rocker along the lines of 'Rock'N'Roll Star'. Good stuff.

DEFINITELY MAYHEM

IT wasn't all good news during late summer and early autumn '94, however. In October, the *NME* ran a live review from the band's American tour at Los Angeles' Whiskey-A-

Two Japanese fans clearly in awe of 'The Brothers'

Go-Go entitled 'Definitely Mayhem' that indicated all was not well in the Oasis camp, pinpointing the shambolic nature of their performance, as well as the tension between audience and band.

The same week, there was a news story suggesting 'Oasis' future was temporarily in doubt after rumours that Noel Gallagher had left the band following a furious row with brother Liam during their American tour.'

Noel's 'disappearance' meant Oasis were forced to cancel shows in Austin, Dallas, Kansas and Missouri. A US spokesman for the band offered 'band fatigue' as the official reason for the cancellations.

There was even worse crowd-band rivalry back home two months before when Noel was attacked onstage by an audience member during Oasis' set at Newcastle's Riverside on August 9th. Tension had gathered all evening with football chants such as 'Man City, wank wank wank' (Oasis love Man City) and 'Soft as shite' being directed at the group.

At first, Noel couldn't work out why things blew up that night in the way they did and the stranger attacked him, he just said: 'We didn't stop and ask him, we just kicked his fuckin' arse, threw him outside and went backstage. I had blood all over the place, there was no way I was going back. My guitar was trashed anyway cos I hit the cunt on the back of the head with it.

'We had to drive out that gig down a sidestreet with three hundred people lined up along the pavement,' he continued, 'and they just smashed the van to bits. Why play for a load of fuckin' monkeys, man? Hopefully all this'll pass.'

Later on, however, Noel put the incident down to the aggressive nature of the song they were playing at the time, 'Bring It Down'.

'It incites violence,' he said. 'That song and "Fade Away" are the two punk songs in the set, and it always gets pretty hairy when we play them. But I never thought it would come to somebody standing up onstage and giving me a black eye.

'There was no forewarning,' he went on. 'Usually you'll get one person in the audience who'll stand there and call you a wanker all night. But this was the first gig in a long time where that hadn't happened. Nothing had been thrown onstage and nobody had spat at us. The next thing we know, I've got this massive cut down the side of my face! I didn't realise that I'd been cut until someone gave me this wet towel and said, "You'd better put that on your eye". I said, "Why?" Then I looked at my shirt and there was blood all over it.'

Assessing the band's growing Mancunian hard-nut reputation later on that night, Noel Gallagher said: 'We're not about fighting, we just want to play our songs. But if someone gets up and thinks he's hard, then he's going to get it.'

The following morning, the *Daily Mirror* reacted with typically magnificent tabloid calm to the incident.

Fret it be!

'Oasis sunk by fans' bloodbath!' screamed the headline of their story, going on: 'Top rockers Oasis were forced to cancel a sell-out show in Newcastle amid an orgy of violence.'

The rival *Daily Star* picked up the baton when, in a two-page feature imaginatively entitled 'SEX'N'DRUGS'N'ROCK'N'ROLL', they ran a detailed portrayal of Oasis as 'The Frightening Five'.

'They're the wildest and most outrageous rock band since The Who launched their notorious orgies of mayhem and destruction,' frothed the *Daily Star*'s John Poole, a man who clearly hasn't been out much these past few decades. 'Shattered hotel rooms, bloody brawls, drugs and groupies are all part of everyday life for these Manchester council estate toughies.

Top, Oasis in Osaka, Japan, September '94. Bottom, in bed with Liam, Nagoya, Japan

Noel grabs a root beer on Route 95, New Jersey

★★★★★★★★★★★★★★★★★★★★

'Whatever'
'I'm free to be whatever I choose'

'Oi, you! Outside – now!' Liam takes on Brighton, December '94

America, less eager to embrace Britain's Next Big Things, respond to Oasis . . . Japan treat the band like they are the new Beatles . . . 'Whatever' narrowly misses the Christmas Number One slot . . . Oasis win numerous awards at the end of the year, and Best Newcomers at Brits '95 . . .

Cambridge, December '94

FOREIGN AFFAIRS

HAVING established themselves as the best new band in Britain, Oasis spent the latter half of 1994 proving they were no parochial UK hype.

First, they consolidated their summer US success, a continent whose music-listening public has, over the years, learned to be suspicious of any Next Big Thing from England, the latter a country with a reputation for, as the cliché goes, building 'em up and knocking 'em down, often managing both within the short space of twelve months.

It was this natural supicion that led to dismal attempts to Make It Big Stateside over the the last decade by the likes of Frankie Goes To Hollywood, The Smiths, The Stone Roses, Happy Mondays and Suede, and the signs were that Oasis would have equal difficulty convincing the relatively conservative American press and public that they were more than just another fey and faddish 'British Haircut Band'.

A typical example of sceptical American press appeared in the *Los Angeles Times* in September: 'Oasis are just another perfectly gratifying but fairly mediocre pop outfit with fab sunglasses and mod hairdos.'

Noel Gallagher had a theory as to why Oasis were going to crack the States, as opposed to, say, Blur or Suede, who were too Anglocentric, even Londoncentric, what with all their preoccupations with going down the dog tracks at Walthamstow (Blur) or eccentric, sexually ambiguous songs about pantomime horses (Suede), whereas Oasis addressed more universal concerns, to whit: Sex, Drugs, Cigarettes, Alcohol, Youth, Relationships, Marriage, Boredom, Freedom, Rebellion and Rock'N'Roll.

This writer had his own (brilliantly original) theory regarding the likelihood of Oasis appealing to America, one that I expressed in an interview with the *Washington Post* in October.

'Traditionally,' I pontificated to the *Post* journalist (actually *MM*'s own Paul Mathur using a pseudonym!), in my official capacity as *Melody Maker* Features Editor and therefore Person Very Slightly Responsible For Breaking Oasis, 'American bands are only ever any good at rock, while British groups are better at pop – and America doesn't really like pop. Unlike the very poppy Blur and Suede – not an ounce of rock in their bodies – Oasis are well-placed because their music lies exactly at the halfway point between rock and pop. That will ensure their music will be enjoyed by yer average American rock fan.'

Actually, it is probably too early to say whether or not Oasis are going to go supernova U2-style in the States - America is far bigger and, therefore, takes far longer to submit to new sensations than Britain - but the fact is that 'Definitely Maybe' has sold many, many thousands of copies Stateside.

Then there's Japan.

Japan took approximately five minutes to submit to Oasis' charms. Mens magazine *GQ* followed the band to Tokyo in September '94 and discovered that, for today's young Japanese, Oasis are the new Fab Four.

'As the Oasis tour bus noses its way out of traffic into a neon-lit side street, an ear-splitting shriek, louder than a wail of feedback, rips through the air,' wrote *GQ* journalist Daniela Soave. 'Hundreds of girls hurtle towards the vehicle, pounding on its windows, rocking it from side to side . . . Oasis have provoked mass hysteria in the normally restrained Japanese fans. I could be witnessing the second coming.'

Southampton, November 1994

Liam Gallagher: the frontman . . .

. . .with the most front

OH WELL, WHATEVER

IN December 1994, the words 'inexorable' and 'rise' kept springing to mind whenever the subject of Oasis cropped up. Because that was the month Oasis enjoyed their fifth hit single in nine months, with a record that only missed being the Christmas Number One by two places, thanks to a bunch of bum-fluffed saccharine rappers from Walthamstow called East 17 and a lachrymose Yuletide ballad screeched by a chubby-faced American harridan called Mariah Carey.

'Whatever', the single in question and the first not to be lifted from 'Definitely Maybe', also only just narrowly missed being the second Oasis record to cause a major legal rumpus in nine months. Because – and this is apart from the public uproar caused by the fact that 'Whatever' sounds more like The Beatles than The Beatles – early copies of the song that did the rounds during the last couple of months of '94 featured a line that went 'All the young blues' and bore such a remarkable melodic resemblance to Mott The Hoople's 'All The Young Dudes' that David Bowie, composer of '. . . Dudes', was rumoured to be threatening to sue Oasis.

When 'Whatever' did come out, on December 19th – timed to perfection to coincide with the last singles chart of the year, the one traditionally known as 'The

Guigsy gives it some bass

Oasis perform 'Shakermaker' on *Top Of The Pops*, June '94

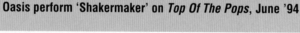

Noel on the video set for 'Whatever'

Christmas Chart' – the 'offending' line had been removed, nixing the band's chances of being involved in a protracted courtroom wrangle with David Bowie. Shame.

The single, described by Noel Gallagher earlier in the year as 'the greatest song ever written' (and only he knows how close his tongue was to his cheek at the time), did, however, reach Number Three in the charts, an especially impressive feat considering the competitive nature of the Top 40 at that time of year. 'Whatever' has since sold in excess of 200,000 copies and is, at the time of writing (early February), still in the Top 20, further proof that Oasis have Crossed Over (singles by 'indie' bands usually enter the charts for one week only to disappear without trace the following week after all the hardcore fans have bought them).

Apart from its affecting 'Abbey Road'-era strings and singalongachorus as well as the obligatory Single Of The Week accolades in *NME* ('The best single of 1994') and *MM* ('Single Of The Fuckin' Year, mate'), the success of 'Whatever' was also helped by Oasis performing it on *Later With Jools Holland*, a TV appearance that surely endeared the band to fortysomething rockers in viewerland who hadn't heard a new record for years but wanted something that took them back to the halcyon days of The Beatles and the Stones.

The extra tracks on the EP couldn't have done much harm, either, not least because at least one of them, '(It's Good) To Be Free', was almost up there with 'Slide Away' for sheer poignant rock ballad perfection. Coincidentally, 'Slide Away' was on the flip of 'Whatever', too, as was 'Half The World Away', yet another acoustic paean to

Backstage at *Top Of The Pops*, December '94

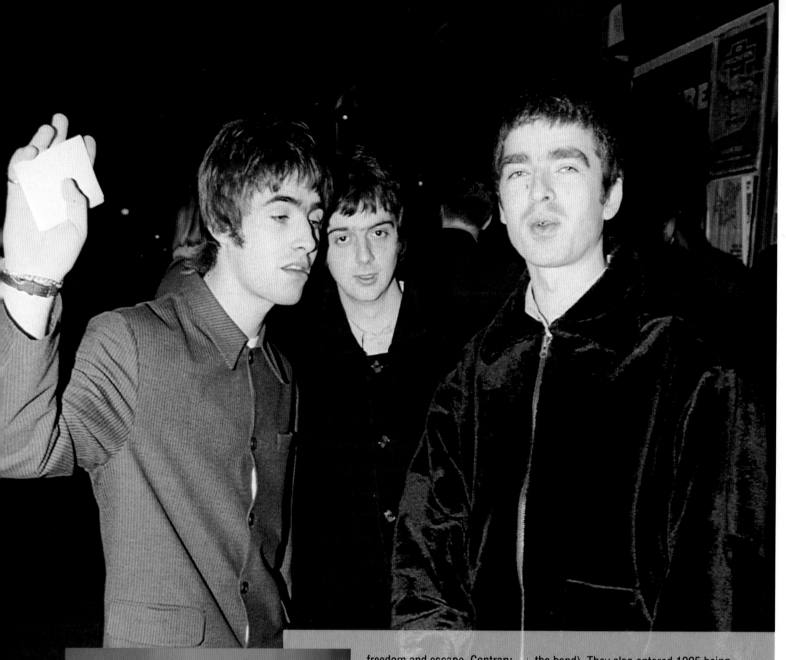

The Brats and the Brits: Oasis outside the *NME* 'Brats' event (top) at which they scooped three awards, and (bottom) being presented with the Best Newcomers award by Kink Ray Davies at the annual music industry Brits Awards, February '95

freedom and escape. Contrary to reports in the music press, the introspective, Kurt Cobain-if-he'd-gone-solo-ish 'Talk Tonight' (Liam: 'The one Noel wrote while he was in San Francisco with some fuckin' bird, that's shit and I fuckin' hate it') and 'Live By The Sea' (Liam: 'Dead heavy, that one Very good') were not on the 'Whatever' EP.

Oasis ended 1994 with a clutch of Best Album/Single/Band Of The Year awards from a huge cross-section of magazine writers, and they won a variety of categories in the *Melody Maker* readers' poll (including Lip Of The Year, for Liam, and Hype Of The Year for

the band). They also entered 1995 being nominated for several Brits as well as numerous Brats, the alternative awards ceremony organised by the *NME*. In the latter they topped the Readers' Poll for Best New Band and Best Single (Live Forever), and 'Definitely Maybe' was voted Album of the Year by *NME* journalists.

Then in February the band was recognised in the annual Brits awards, the flagship event for the British recording industry, trouncing their rivals in the Best Newcomers category.

So there you have it. Oasis: not just the best new band in Britain, but also the hardest new band in Britain.

Only bullets - or a bad record - can stop them now.

Diary Of A Mad Rock Band

The rise and rise of Oasis, Britain's five-year overnight sensations

1989:-

October: A seminal moment for the whole baggy/'Madchester' scene and the highpoint for wannabe Mancunian pop stars when The Stone Roses and Happy Mondays slouch and slur their way through 'Fools Gold' and 'Hallelujah', on *Top Of The Pops*.

1990:-

April: Liam and Noel Gallagher from Burnage, a suburb of South Manchester, attend a hometown show by The Stone Roses which has an enormous impact on the brothers. Afterwards, Noel meets Clint Boon of Inspiral Carpets, who is bootlegging the gig. Noel asks Clint to send him a copy. The pair soon become friends and, as the Inspirals find success on the back of the 'Madchester' bandwagon, Noel quits his job at British Gas to be the Inspirals' guitar tech-cum-roadie.

1991:-

August: While on tour with the Inspirals, Noel phones home only to be told by his mother that brother Liam has formed a band with old friends Tony McCarroll, Paul McGuigan and Paul 'Bonehead' Arthurs (all formerly of The Rain, though not to be confused with the Liverpudlian baggy chancers of the same name). The band are to be called Oasis.

1992:-

January: Back from a world tour (Russia, America, Argentina, Japan) with the Carpets, Noel decides to check out Oasis at Manchester's Boardwalk. He later says it was 'an opportunity staring me in the face'. He tells Oasis that they are 'shite' and that only one thing will improve their fortunes – let him take over as songwriter and guitarist. Noel plays them three of his songs. Liam and co agree that Noel should be band leader.

March-December: Noel continues to roadie for the Inspirals. In his spare time and during soundchecks, he writes songs, all the time knowing 'I was miles better than the Inspirals – miles better.' Eventually, Noel leaves the Inspirals to concentrate on Oasis.

Oasis get their rocks off at the Astoria

1993:-

January-May: Oasis hawk their wares around the live circuit to very little attention or acclaim.

May: Oasis travel to Glasgow with Manchester's all-girl Sister Lovers and are booked to support Creation Records' 18 Wheeler at King Tut's Wah Wah Club. Oasis threaten the club owner with violence if they're not allowed to play. They do play, Creation boss Alan McGee, there by chance, sees Oasis, hails them the future of rock'n'roll and tries to sign them on the spot.

June: A cheaply-recorded Oasis demo does the rounds in Manchester. Former Smiths guitarist Johnny Marr hears it and, impressed, proceeds to get his own management company to sign the band after watching them support Dodgy. Marr also gives Noel his Gibson Les Paul guitar, one formerly owned by The Who's Pete Townshend.

August: The first Oasis live review appears in the weekly music press. The *NME*'s Emma Morgan, reviewing them at the Boardwalk, calls them 'the shoots of vitality in a barren pop land'.

'Did you call my pint a poof?'

September: *Melody Maker*'s Paul Mathur, a key figure in the band's success, reviews the band at Manchester's 'In The City' festival alongside Creation's 18 Wheeler and Medalark 11 ('the beautifully arrogant power of youth').

October: Despite allegedly massive six-figure advances from at least 20 record companies, Oasis finally sign to Sony worldwide, via Creation in Britain.

November: In the band's first ever interview,

November-December: Oasis tour once more, this time supporting Verve, Liz Phair, Milltown Brothers, St Etienne, Real People and 'other shit bands' (Noel Gallagher).

December: Creation send out a teaser to selected press and radio stations: a one-sided white label promo 12-inch of 'Columbia' from the band's demo tape, the first song Oasis ever performed in front of an audience. Radio 1FM playlist it – an unprecedented move.

1994:-

January: Oasis enter Liverpool's Pink Museum studios. In eight hours, they write and record 'Supersonic', due to be their debut single. The initial album sessions are less successful, and after two days at the rural £800-a-day Monnow Studios, all they have to show are some ragged Rolling Stones covers. Inter-band friction leads to the sessions being aborted.

January: In *Melody Maker*, Oasis reveal their favourite artists to be The Beatles, David Bowie, The Stooges, Paul Weller, Captain Beefheart and, slightly more up-to-date, Grant Lee Buffalo.

January: The band play their debut London gig at the Water Rats, King's Cross, a low-key, invites-only affair. 200 people have to be turned away.

February: After yet more disastrous LP sessions at the famous Olympic Studios in Barnes, the band start again from scratch down at Cornwall's Sawmills Studios with Mark Coyle (who Noel knew from his Inspirals days) and Anjali Dutt at the controls. The album is completed in ten days, with just the mixing and arranging to be done elsewhere by Electronic's producer, Owen Morris.

February: Oasis' reputation for brattish rock'n'roll behaviour starts when, on the ferry to Amsterdam to play support to Verve, Noel disembarks and the rest of the band reputedly get drunk, brawl and smash furniture. They are promptly deported by the Dutch authorities.

March: Oasis' other extra-curricular reputation, for fraternal imbroglios, begins during their first co-headlining tour (with Whiteout) when a Southampton gig is curtailed after Noel allegedly punched Liam and then chased him offstage.

March: The band transfix audiences with their debut TV appearance, on Channel 4's *The Word*, a performance of soon-to-come debut single 'Supersonic'. They also get arrested after a 100 Club gig because the police thought they 'looked dodgy'. The band were released after giving the fuzz signed copies of 'Supersonic'.

Nagoya, Japan, September 1994

Oasis tell *MM*'s Paul Mathur they're more than just another Manchester band.

November: In the *NME*'s gossip column, 'Public NME', Oasis' Noel and Paul are accused of beating up Liam, Tony and Bonehead for jamming onstage with Whiteout at the Camden Falcon without them, a sign of in-fighting to come . . .

December: The backlash has started already! *NME*'s Johnny Cigarettes calls Liam a 'vaguely Ian Brown-as-Tim Burgess slob of a frontman'. Liam will later threaten to deck the hack, although not to his face. To redress the critical balance, in *G Spot* magazine Paul Mathur says Oasis are 'the best new group in Britain'.

Oasismania at the 100 Club

April: 'Supersonic' is released. The general public buy enough copies to send it sailing to Number 31 while the *NME* make it Single Of The Week and interview Liam and Noel, the pair filling the hapless hack's tape with petty sniping.

April: Oasis are escorted off Stonehenge after climbing the fence and threatening to 'reclaim the historic monument for the people', and Noel reveals that he has a song, 'All Around The World' (not the Barry White/Lisa Stansfield tune), that will one day win the Eurovision Song Contest.

May: Oasis undertake their first, sell-out headline tour. *Select* readers are treated to a cassette featuring the Sixties-influenced 'Fade Away'.

June: Oasis perform at 'Undrugged', the 10th anniversary of Creation at the Royal Albert Hall and preview forthcoming singles 'Shakermaker', 'Live Forever' and 'Whatever'.

June: 'Shakermaker' (Single Of The Week in *MM* and *NME*) is released to some

controversy due to its half-inching the melody from an ancient Coca-Cola theme. The single crashes into the Top 20, eventually reaching Number 11, and the band make their debut *Top Of The Pops* appearance. They also perform on Channel Four's *Naked City*. Further proof that Oasis are making an impact outside the music press comes in the form of major articles in the style magazines (*Sky, The Face, iD*).

June: The band make their festival debut at Glastonbury. 'Are you gonna wake up for some real songs?' Liam goads the blissed-out hordes. The next night, the band become only the third ever (after The Fall and The Mission) to be banned from London's most famous rock'n'roll hotel, The Columbia, after trashing it. The *NME* put Oasis on the front: 'What The World Is Waiting For', says the cover line.

July: Noel joins his hero Neil Young's backing band, Crazy Horse, onstage at London's King's College, where they are

playing with former Icicle Works man, Ian McNabb. 'My mum's dead proud of me!' beams Noel.

July: Oasis head off to New York to play the annual New Music Seminar alongside Britpop talent Echobelly, These Animal Men, S*M*A*S*H and Kaliphz and film a video in Central Park for third single 'Live Forever', all of which is detailed in the first *Melody Maker* cover story on the band by longtime Oasis aficionado, Paul Mathur.

July: Oasis play the 'T In The Park' festival in Strathclyde.

August: 'Live Forever' enters the charts at Number Ten as Oasis set off for the Hultsfred Festival in Sweden, where there are numerous hotel bar antics, members of the band arrested and reports that Liam has managed to break his foot while jumping off the tour bus.

August: Noel is punched in the face while onstage at Newcastle's Riverside by an audience member. 'An orgy of violence!' screams the *Daily Mirror*.

August: The band's first album, 'Definitely Maybe', is released to universal acclaim – even hardcore dance 'zine *Mixmag* gives it 10 out of 10. It is also the fastest-selling debut LP of all time, selling 150,000 copies in three days. It effortlessly enters the chart at pole position.

August: The band perform an acoustic instore performance at London's Virgin Megastore and are joined, unexpectedly, by flaxen-haired crack'n'slacker rock god, Evan Dando of The Lemonheads, who proclaims himself Oasis' biggest fan.

September: An epochal cross-generational moment occurs when Liam and Pete Townshend meet at an airport while reading about each other in different magazines. And an epochal cross-artistic moment occurs when Paul 'Guigsy' McGuigan chooses his dream Man City team in soccer mag *90 Minutes*.

September: Oasis play Manchester's Hacienda and are supported by cult Sixties faves, the Creation. *Vox* magazine calls it the city's finest moment since the height of 'Madchester'. The band also undertake a short tour of Japan, which is sold out – in true post-Beatles fashion – in a matter of a few days.

October: Oasis release the hedonists' anthem 'Cigarettes & Alcohol', which climbs to Number 7 even though it's the fourth single to be lifted from 'Definitely Maybe'. The record's high chart position is helped by *Top Of The Pops* showing the band's black and white video. Meanwhile, in *Vox* Liam decries Damon from Blur for not being a lad and tells lad Bible, *Loaded*, that John Lennon

Liam outstares all-comers

Glastonbury '94

is the most famous person, alive or dead, he'd like to shag.

October: Granada TV air their *With Oasis* documentary, with footage from the Buckley Tivoli and Virgin Megastore as well as interviews with Liam and Noel.

October: Following a live *NME* review from their American tour that points towards increasing inter-band tension, rumours circulate that Noel is to leave Oasis. The rumours are quashed by Oasis and Creation.

November: The *Daily Mirror* indicates that Noel has fallen in love with MTV presenter Rebecca De Ruvo and Oasis feature in

fashion Bible, *Vogue*. Meanwhile, Oasis tour Europe, playing the Les Inrockuptibles festival in Paris with Britpop peers Shed Seven, Elastica, Gene and Echobelly. *Melody Maker* print a news story alleging that the band urinated in a hotel corridor, which the band and record company strenuously deny.

November: News reports confirm that 'Whatever' will be Oasis' fifth single, their first not to be lifted from 'Definitely Maybe'.

December: Oasis cut short a gig at Glasgow's Barrowlands after Liam punches his mic in frustration at losing his voice. Meanwhile, the *Daily Mirror* reports that Noel

Brighton fans, June 1994

Noel showing off his new Pontiac

Noel and Evan luvvy it up, Dublin, September '94

is homeless and Oasis are nominated for three prestigious Brit Awards – Best British Band, Best British Newcomer and Best British Album.

December: Oasis offer a sneak live preview – plus full string section – of the highly ambitious version of 'Whatever' on the last episode of Jools Holland's highly successful *Later* television series.

December: 'Whatever' is released. Once again, Oasis are *NME/MM* Single Of The Week. Months after bookies started taking

Board Game'. Also in NME, a musicologist points to the folk roots of Noel Gallagher's compositions. As for Melody Maker, it decides that Oasis, along with Blur, Pulp and the Manic Street Preachers, are band of the year, while Vox chooses 'Supersonic' as its Single Of The Year.

1995:-

January: Oasis are up for numerous 'Brats' awards (*NME*'s alternative to the Brits) – Best LP, Best New Band, Best Single, Best

NME's Brats ceremony - where Oasis pick up awards for Best Single ('Live Forever'), Best New Band as well as Best Band – squaring up with various unknowns and generally causing an affray.

February: *Vox* details the exact number of Oasis gigs in 1994 – 120 – and their biggest performing date so far – the 30,000-plus crowd at Glastonbury. At the end of the month they scoop the Best Newcomers accolade at the Brit Awards.

March: Oasis tour the States once more.

The Glastonbury Festival, June 1994

odds and offering 30/1 on Oasis being the Christmas Number One, the band's fifth single misses the coveted Yuletide pole position by just two places, pipped at the post by singer Mariah Carey and teeny-fave vocal group East 17.

December: The Vox and NME critics vote 'Definitely Maybe' Album Of The Year, the latter rag calling it 'the mightiest debut since "The Stone Roses"' and inventing 'The Oasis

Gig and Best Band. *Smash Hits* magazine describes Noel as nothing less than 'a songwriting genius'.

January: The readers of *Melody Maker* vote 'Live Forever' and 'Supersonic' as their Singles Of The Year, Liam as their Lip Of The Year and Oasis as Hype Of The Year. *Mojo*, the magazine for Stones/Beatles/Dylan/ Hendrix buffs, proclaims 'Definitely Maybe' to be 'the story of 1994'. Liam gets rowdy at

April: Oasis release their brand new single entitled 'Some May Say' (with the B-side, 'Talk Tonight', finally available after months of it circulating as an 'official' bootleg on tapes heard only by friends and close family). Oasis' sixth single evinces a marked shift away from the now familiar Beatles/Stones sound – instead, it has a swaggering almost sing-along chorus worthy of Rod Stewart and The Faces.

Noel and Co sign their lives away at the Heineken Festival *Melody Maker* signing tent

23 SONGS THAT SHOOK THE WORLD!

(Every Oasis song ever committed to cassette/vinyl/CD)

1. 'Supersonic' (available as a single and on the 'Definitely Maybe' album)
2. 'Take Me Away' (extra track on seven-inch and CD singles)
3. 'I Will Believe' (live track on 12-inch and CD singles)
4. 'Columbia' (demo available on the CD single; studio version on LP)
5. 'Shakermaker' (single, available on all formats; also on LP)
6. 'D'Yer Wanna Be A Spaceman?' (extra track on all formats)
7. 'Alive' (8-track demo on the 12-inch and CD singles)
8. 'Bring It On Down' (live track on CD and on free *Vox* tape, 'K-Vox Blasting The Airwaves'; studio version on LP)
9. 'Live Forever' (all formats single; also on LP)
10. 'Up In The Sky' (acoustic track, all formats; full band version on LP)
11. 'Cloudburst' (an extra track on 12-inch and CD)
12. 'Rock'N'Roll Star' (album track; also on free *Vox* tape, 'Class Of '94')
13. 'Digsy's Dinner' (album track)
14. 'Slide Away' (album track; also on 12-inch of 'Whatever' and free *Q* magazine CD, 'Really Free')
15. 'Married With Children' (album track)
16. 'Sad Song' (extra track only available on double LP vinyl version of 'Definitely Maybe')
17. 'Cigarettes & Alcohol' (album track and single, all formats)
18. 'I Am The Walrus' (live track, all formats)
19. 'Fade Away' (12-inch and CD only; also on free *Select* magazine tape, 'Secret Tracks 2')
20. 'Listen Up' (CD single only)
21. 'Whatever' (all formats single)
22. '(It's Good) To Be Free' (extra track on all formats)
23. 'Half The World Away' (extra track on CD only)

PLUS! THE ONES THAT GOT AWAY . . .

(Four Oasis songs that nearly made it onto cassette/vinyl/CD)

1. 'Talk Tonight': a maudlin, bluesy solo number from Noel on which his voice sounds uncannily like Kurt Cobain's.
2. 'Take Me': a song from Liam Gallagher, the man apparently responsible for 'Columbia' – this is equally raunchy and ragged.
3. 'Whatever I': the original version of 'Whatever', this one featured the line, 'All the young blues' and bore such a striking melodic resemblance to David Bowie's composition for Mott The Hoople, 'All The Young Dudes', that the band decided it might be wise to whip out the offending section.
4. 'Strange Thing': recorded at the Pink Museum, this is pure Oasis-play-The Faces in a psychedelic-punk stylee.